Macdonald Careers

Department Store

Gerald Whiting

Macdonald Educational

Editor Elisabeth Edwards
Design Robert Wheeler
Production Susan Mead
Picture Research Brigitte Arora

First published in 1979 by
Macdonald Educational Ltd.
Holywell House
Worship Street
London EC2A2EN
© Macdonald Educational 1979

ISBN 0-382-06356-2

Published in the United
States by Silver Burdett
Company, Morristown, N.J.
1979 Printing

Library of Congress
Catalog Card No. 79-67166

Arthur D'Arazien, From Shostal Associates

Contents

A department store

The first department stores were built by enterprising people who realized the need for shops which sold 'everything under one roof', as they so often boasted. They gradually expanded their small, one-man businesses by buying up the houses and shops on either side until they had achieved their goal – an island site, with entrances and windows all round and a road on each side.

Early department stores were very different from those today, both for the customers and for the assistants, who slept over the shop and had to clean it before it opened each day. The windows were crammed with goods, with little or no attempt at selection or display. On entering, the customer was greeted by a floorwalker in morning dress, who ushered her to a chair and asked what she would like to see.

'Show me the latest hats, please.'

'Certainly, modom. Miss Jones! Bring modom this season's hats!'

Buying anything could take a very long time. There was no self-service, all the goods being brought to the customer by the assistants from shelves or drawers behind the polished wood counters. Money was either rung up on jangling cash registers or put, with the bill, into small metal tubes hanging from wires above the counters. These ran to the cashier's desk, behind a grille in the centre of the department. She put the change and the receipt into the tube and sent it flying back across the room to the assistant. Purchases were elaborately wrapped before being carried to the customer's carriage.

Today's department stores are far more streamlined and efficient in the numbers of goods and customers they handle. However, they retain their original purpose – they sell everything.

A large store today trades in a basement below street-level, on the ground floor itself and on four, five or even more floors above that. Yet for every square metre of sales floors there is about as much again elsewhere. There are stockrooms in the sub-basement and behind partitions throughout the store. On the highest floors are management and other offices and the staff amenities such as dining rooms, rest rooms, medical rooms. Many stores also have a roof garden.

With over 1,500 people on its pay roll, only half of whom will be visible to the public on the sales floor, a big department store has a community life of its own and hundreds of different jobs for people with a variety of interests and abilities.

Main entrance

In a large department store there would be:
20,000 square metres of flooring, about half of which would be selling space;
enough carpeting for 150 three-bedroomed houses and enough hard floor coverings for 150 more;
12 entrances through which over 30,000 people would pass each day, rising to over 100,000 at peak times;
a staff restaurant serving about 1300 coffees, 1300 teas and 100 lunches daily;
while its 12 delivery vans would cover 1500 kilometres a day making 500 deliveries – 130,000 in a year.

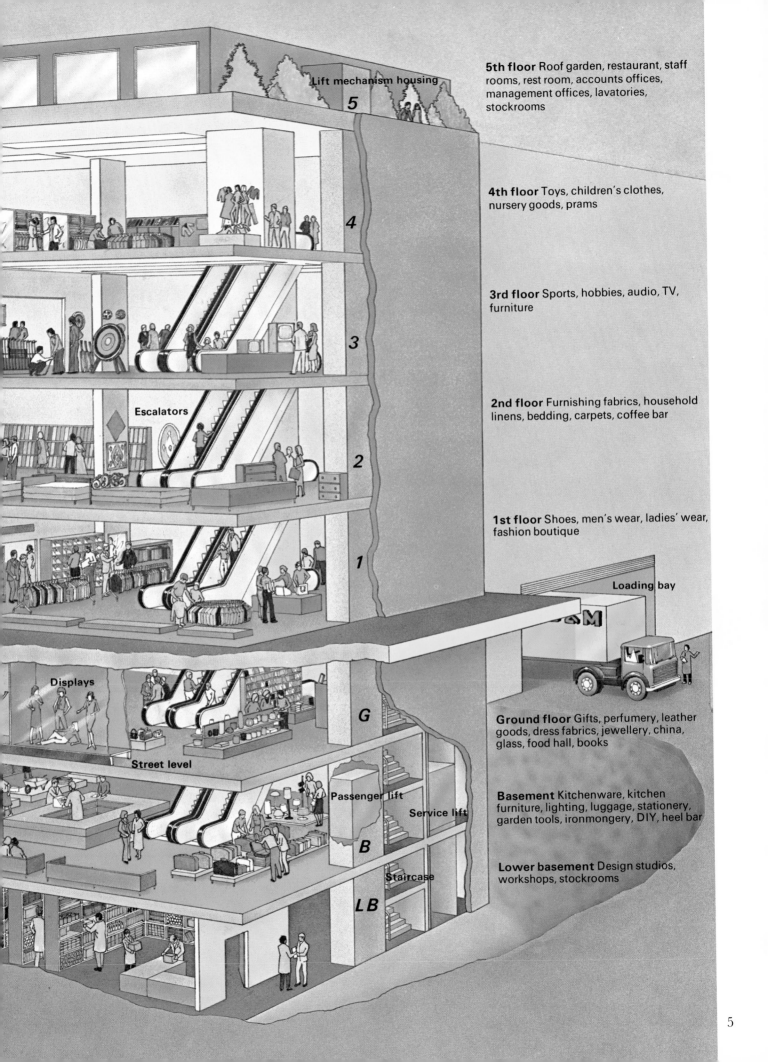

5th floor Roof garden, restaurant, staff rooms, rest room, accounts offices, management offices, lavatories, stockrooms

Lift mechanism housing

5

4

4th floor Toys, children's clothes, nursery goods, prams

3

3rd floor Sports, hobbies, audio, TV, furniture

Escalators

2

2nd floor Furnishing fabrics, household linens, bedding, carpets, coffee bar

1st floor Shoes, men's wear, ladies' wear, fashion boutique

1

Loading bay

Displays

G

Street level

Passenger lift

Service lift

B

Staircase

LB

Ground floor Gifts, perfumery, leather goods, dress fabrics, jewellery, china, glass, food hall, books

Basement Kitchenware, kitchen furniture, lighting, luggage, stationery, garden tools, ironmongery, DIY, heel bar

Lower basement Design studios, workshops, stockrooms

5

Coming to life

A day in the life of a department store starts early. By night it is a fortress guarded by watchmen and an elaborate security alarm system. Steel shutters are wound down when the shop closes to seal off the sales floors from the outer staircases. The location of an intruder or a fire is flashed up immediately on the central control panel in the security office. At the same time an alert goes out automatically to the nearest police and fire stations. This vigilance is vital, for the shop and its stock are worth millions of pounds.

6.15 The first of the kitchen staff arrive so that other early arrivals can have breakfast or hot drinks.

6.30 Several maintenance men and all the cleaners are collecting keys from the watchmen's box before starting work in the offices and several kilometres of corridors.

6.45 The internal shutters are raised, revealing departments still shrouded in dust sheets. The van yard opens and the first of the day's deliveries arrives for unloading and checking while the streets are still fairly free from traffic. Roughly half of the deliveries are from the department store's out-of-town warehouse about fifteen kilometres away. The rest come directly from individual suppliers of anything from fashions to furniture and paper napkins; from kitchen gadgets to glassware and television sets.

7.30 The display teams are at work, moving new display material to the windows through the still empty shop and taking out the old for disposal or for storage until it is needed again. Each section of window display, called window-run, is changed weekly and, if possible, before the store is open.

8.00 With sixty minutes to go before opening time the departments are already full of activity. The cleaners are moving through with large industrial polishers and smaller vacuum cleaners; two maintenance men are working on a lift which was operating too slowly the day before and electricians are installing some new spotlights. A few of the hundred or so section managers have come in early with one or two members of their staff. They are checking the stock or perhaps making a minor re-arrangement of the department to improve the flow of customers or to speed the wrapping of the goods they buy.

8.45 The dust covers are being taken off. All the lights are switched on.

8.55 The last of the late arrivals are hurrying to their posts and trying to look as though they have been there for several minutes!

9.00 precisely A security man, watch in hand, unlocks each door. The first fifty or so of the day's one hundred thousand customers hurry in.

▲ A well-lit run of windows full of colourful items is a store's most powerful advertisement. Keeping the windows clean is a daily task. Using long-handled mops and sponges a good team can clean a run of windows thirty metres long and three metres high in about 45 minutes.

▼ Cleaning through a shop is very like cleaning a home, except that much of it has to be done before 9 am! Heavy domestic vacuum cleaners can cope with even the biggest areas of carpeting and move easily round furniture in the offices.

▲ Shop assistants keep their own displays clean and tidy. Dust sheets give general protection, and glass surfaces are kept shining with detergent.

▶ Letting in the customers is a precisely-timed operation. The alarm system is switched off and a security officer at each entrance opens a door simultaneously. Each door has two or more different types of locks or bolts at top and bottom.

▼ Industrial scrubber/polishers like this triple-pad machine are used regularly to give a non-slip buffing to vinyl and other hard floor coverings.

A satisfied customer

It is now mid-morning. The store is beginning to fill with customers on shopping trips from the suburbs. Their numbers will soon be swelled by the lunch-time rush of office workers, usually the busiest time of the day. The sales assistants have finished checking and tidying the stock; the display shelves have been refilled and staff who were taking the second coffee-break are about to return.

By 11.30 business is getting brisk. With luck the store will 'do its figures' which means to equal, if not beat, the sales target for the day. The sales assistants are kept busy as new customers arrive, each with a different need. It is up to the assistant to find out what that need is.

'Your little girl seems very taken with that green dress. Is it for something special?'

'Yes, her birthday party. But it's rather expensive for just one occasion. Will it wash?'

'It will, but only if you have time to do it by hand. . . It looks nice on you, dear, but what do you like most about it? The colour or the shape?'

'The shape really, and these sleeves.'

'Well, let's see now. There's something very like it over here in a lovely brushed nylon which will wash very easily. Why don't you try that on too? It matches your eyes. . .'

Downstairs in the audio department a customer is asking the RMS value of a music centre's twin speakers. The assistant is beginning a general discussion of technicalities that will tell him whether the customer really knows his subject or whether he has just picked up an isolated piece of information. He will also try to find out the circumstances in which the equipment will be used and whether an extendable system built up from separate units might suit the customer better.

An assistant in the toy department is helping a teenage girl to choose a model aircraft for her eight-year-old brother.

'I can see why he'd like a fighter plane but it's not a beginner's model. This high-winger flies very well and is much easier to build.'

'My father would help him, I think. It used to be one of his hobbies.'

'Ah well, there's no problem then. The fighter kit is complete except for this set of camouflage paints. Would you like them included?'

'Yes, please. And thank you for being so helpful.'

The sales assistant has to be cheerful, imaginative, understanding and infinitely patient. This is the most visible, and therefore the best known job in retailing. It is also one of the most important, for a satisfied customer will come back again.

◀ Fitting shoes is a highly specialized task. Assistants in children's shoe departments are trained to measure both feet accurately and to make sure that the shoes fit correctly.

▶ The assistants in sports departments are often athletes, swimmers, tennis players or golfers themselves. Their own interests help them to give customers good advice in choosing equipment. The sales assistant's job is not to sell the most expensive item but the one most suitable for the customer.

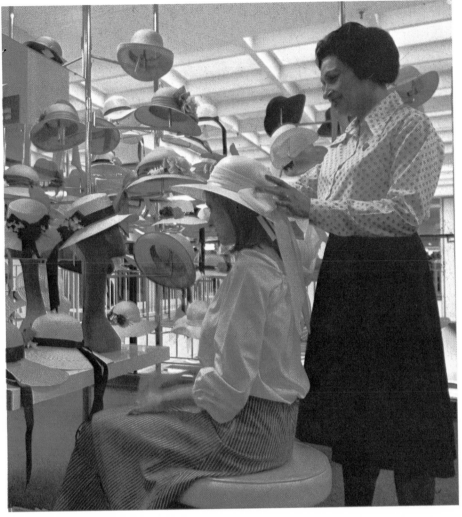

▲ Records and cassette tapes are often sold in or near the audio equipment department. Booths and headphones allow customers to listen to recordings without distractions. Assistants working here need to be interested in a wide range of music, from classical to pop.

▲ Hats are often bought for special occasions, such as weddings. A good assistant will find this out in general conversation and then select hats which suit the customer.

▶ Each perfumery house has its own area of counter, staffed by beauty consultants who are trained to assess each customer's needs and to advise her on the choice of cosmetics from the house's products.

The sales team

The members of a sales team, particularly those who are in daily contact with the customers, are known as the department store's 'front line troops'. They are appropriately named, for in the brief moments when the customer and the sales assistant meet, the shop's reputation rests solely with the sales assistant. There is no other area in which the basic skills of retailing can be learned in so short a time. Many careers leading to the highest levels of management begin with the thorough training gained in working on the sales floor.

Sales assistant

For those who enjoy meeting and dealing with people this can be an exciting and rewarding job. Many young people decide to remain with the sales team for the rest of their working lives. Others find it — usually after years of varied experience — a way into buying or top management.

There are opportunities for graduates as well as for those with few qualifications.

Every large department store has a training programme or programmes which will help individuals develop greater knowledge and skills. Young people joining straight from school start with a conducted tour of the shop and stock-rooms and a brief introduction to the history of the shop and its trading methods and policies. They meet the manager of the department which they are to join and begin a programme of induction training. This combines practising answering telephone inquiries, making out sales bills and other practical details with actual work in the department and its associated stock-rooms.

Later, individual skills and interests may emerge. For example, a flair for fashion or furnishings, an enthusiasm for electronics or an appreciation of fine china may govern the way in which a young entrant's career will develop.

The next stage of training is usually a two-year programme. It often includes one day a week at a technical college to study for a retail trade certificate and occasional one or two-day training courses within the shop to increase the trainee's knowledge of merchandise, selling techniques, computerised till systems, display methods and so on. It may also be supplemented with planned working experience in several different departments.

The trainee may gravitate naturally towards work in the stockroom, dealing with customer inquiries on the telephone or one of the many other jobs vital to the efficiency of the selling team. Later years will bring opportunities to move into other work for which selling experience is a helpful qualification.

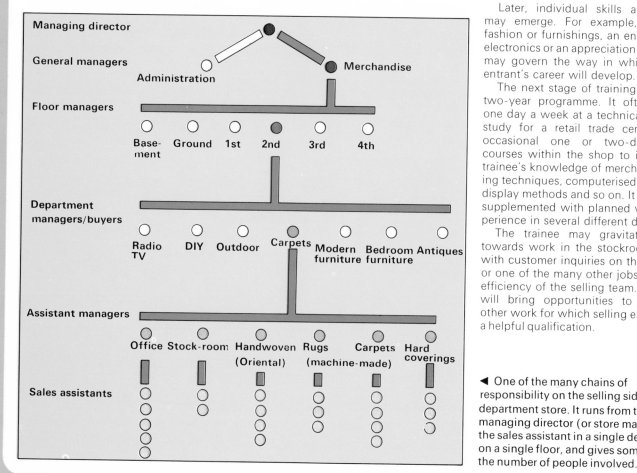

◀ One of the many chains of responsibility on the selling side of a large department store. It runs from the managing director (or store manager) to the sales assistant in a single department on a single floor, and gives some idea of the number of people involved.

Assistant manager

This is the first step on the management ladder. An assistant manager is responsible for one area of a department's operations and is in charge of two or more assistants. Some assistant managers may have entered as juniors and spent many years as sales assistants; others may be comparatively young but highly-qualified and already selected by higher management as suitable for rapid promotion.

Assistant managers will have shown themselves able to work well under pressure; to be able to plan ahead and anticipate problems and to have displayed a degree of judgement and leadership that will enable them to inspire and guide others.

Some assistant managers remain as specialists in one particular area of merchandise like textiles, carpets or furniture. Others may spend time gathering experience in a series of different assistant managerships before further promotion to department manager or department manager/buyer.

Department manager

The power of this position varies with the size of department. An assistant manager in a major department in a large store can earn more than a department manager of a very small one.

The department manager is responsible to the store manager, either directly or through a floor manager, for the efficient running of his department and the well-being of his staff. He will also have an understanding of the organization of the shop or group as a whole.

Department manager/buyer

In many stores and store groups the department managers are responsible not only for running their department efficiently but also for buying the stock sold there. They have firsthand experience of how the goods will be displayed and marketed, which helps when making buying decisions.

Floor manager

A floor manager is responsible to the store manager for all the departments on one floor. She advises on and co-ordinates interior displays affecting one or more departments, and agrees the expansion and contraction of selling areas according to season.

Floor managers are often men or women who are destined eventually for posts in higher management.

▲ At least twice a year every item in each department is checked to make sure that the number in stock agrees with the records of the number sold. This is called stocktaking. Much of it is done after the shop has finished trading for the day.

▶ Sales assistants must be able to assemble and demonstrate any item in their department. They learn how to do this in training sessions with a senior member of the staff, such as the buyer, or with the manufacturer's representative.

▼ A crowded store at its busiest. Thousands of articles are being paid for, wrapped and taken away. Each member of staff contributes to the speed and efficiency of these complex operations.

Enough in stock?

◄Small goods are unpacked and stacked in this four-metre high racking before being repacked in plastic bins to meet orders from the store.

▼ The stockkeeper is responsible for keeping records of everything that enters or leaves the warehouse. Today, much of this work is done by computers.

A big department store stocks several million different items of merchandise – and several million more will be in transit towards it, day and night, by land, sea or air, from most parts of the world. Not all of them will reach it.

One Saturday morning Mrs Pringle finally decided which new refrigerator she would buy. She paid for it and asked for it to be delivered. However, the refrigerator she received a week later had never been in the shop, or even in the stockroom. It was delivered direct from the shop's warehouse, built some distance from the city centre where land was cheaper. If a store is part of a group, its own warehouse may be served by a group warehouse, built even further out in the country.

In one such warehouse serving seventeen department stores there are 500 people who between them handle nearly 30 million units of goods in one year. As many as 150 vans and trailers, some of which are almost four metres long, are unloaded there on a peak day during the pre-Christmas rush. The usual daily rate is about 64, and about 16,500 are unloaded in a year.

There are various handling methods, depending on what has been delivered. Cartons full of small goods like handbags, shoes or china travel up sloping conveyor belts to an upper level where they are unpacked, repacked in plastic bins and put into low racks, less than four metres high. Such goods are sent on to the stores soon, if not immediately, afterwards. The plastic bins are stacked on wheeled bases or in wheeled cages and towed in trains behind small electric tugs to the dispatch bays.

The heavy, bulky items like refrigerators, cookers and furniture arrive on standard-sized wooden platforms called *pallets*. Pallets can be raised on the prongs of a fork-lift truck or on those of a small wheeled device that can be towed by hand. Such items tend to spend longer in storage and are placed in high racks.

Pallets are lifted into place – and retrieved again for dispatch – by order-pickers. The smallest of these are rather like fork-lift trucks but with unusually high lifting mechanisms. These can be driven wherever needed. Others are tall metal columns which move along rails fixed in the aisles between the racks. A cage with a fork attached can be made to rise up or down the column to reach any pallet. In some aisles the operator rides on the machine and picks merchandise by hand. The newer order-pickers are operated by remote control, and the most recent of all solely by computer.

For big department store groups, such warehousing helps to minimise the costs which accumulate with frightening speed if expensive city centre space has to be used for storage instead of for selling goods.

▲ Although the boxes and parcels have been counted and checked against the delivery dockets in the loading bay, each one then has to be unpacked and checked to make sure that the contents tally too.

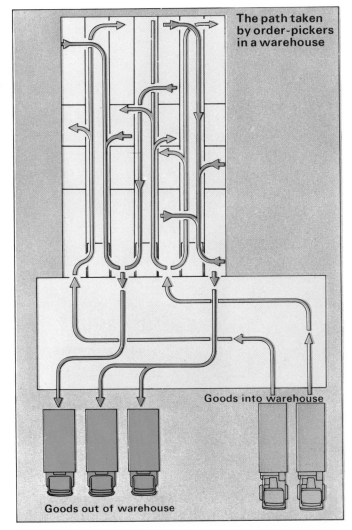

The path taken by order-pickers in a warehouse

Goods into warehouse

Goods out of warehouse

▲ Warehouses have different shelving systems for different goods. They are put into racks and retrieved by machines called order-pickers. Each machine stacks goods as it moves one way along the aisle and retrieves ordered goods as it returns.

▲ This is a manned order-picker, which can stack or retrieve a large load of rolled fabrics from any part of the racking on either side. The racks may be up to seven metres high.

▼ How the selling price of a TV set is made up

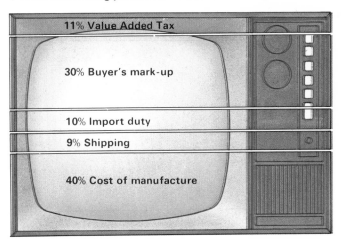

11% Value Added Tax

30% Buyer's mark-up

10% Import duty

9% Shipping

40% Cost of manufacture

▲ Sending goods by sea in large containers is the cheapest way of covering long distances. However, it still accounts for nearly twenty per cent of the selling price of a Japanese television set in a European shop.

The story of a dress

Silkworms are fed on mulberry leaves.

A silk-worm chrysalis inside its cocoon.

The filaments from five to ten cocoons are combined to make one thread.

A dress is designed. Its colour is chosen from the manufacturer's fabric samples.

A sample dress is made up and fitted.

The dresses are packed and loaded on to an airplane.

On arrival, they are delivered to the store's stockroom.

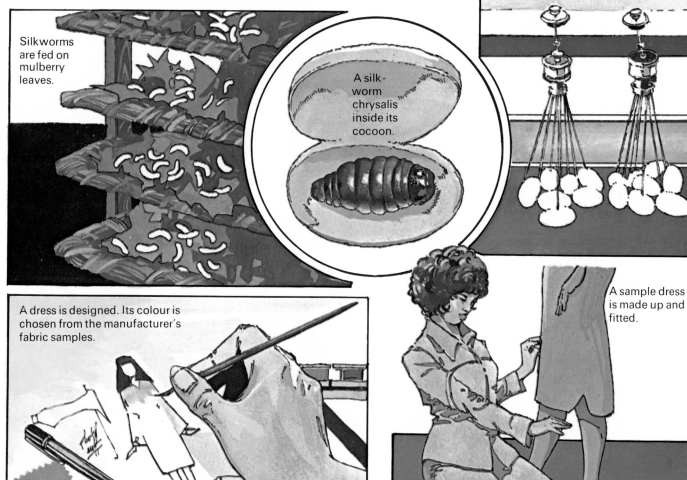

The raw silk thread is woven into cloth, either as it is or after being dyed. Some is still woven by hand, using serrated fingernails to create a raised pattern.

Today, most silk is woven on huge power-looms.

Once a colour or design has been decided, the fabric is dyed or screen-printed.

Fashion buyers select dresses at a parade held by the dress manufacturer.

The buyer's order is made up.

A window-dresser arranges a display, designed around the silk dress.

The fabric designer, fashion designer, buyer and window-dresser are all successful — the dress is selling well.

A buyer's life

I am sorry but we don't seem to have any more blue ones at present. . .' That probably means a lost sale. If the full range can be found in the shop next door, it may also mean a lost customer.

Deciding what goods shall be stocked and in what quantities is the job of the buyer. She also has to decide the price at which the article will sell. A department store buyer may be responsible for one department in one shop or, increasingly nowadays, be a central buyer of one type of merchandise for all the shops in a group.

Buying decisions involve hundreds of thousands of pounds of the firm's money, so mistakes can be disastrous. The buyer must fix prices which are high enough to cover all the costs incurred and to produce a margin of profit, but not so high that the customer will decide to shop elsewhere.

If the goods are likely to sell quickly and in large numbers the buyer may feel able to take a lower profit than on slower moving items which could occupy valuable selling space in the shop for several weeks or months. Such goods are said to have high or low 'stockturns'.

To make such decisions, the buyer must combine a real understanding of customer likes and dislikes with the ability to interpret statistics. The detailed sales analysis which was once written by hand or typed is now more likely to arrive on her desk in the form of large folded sheets printed out from a computer. These show exactly how many of each item has been sold in a certain period, so that the buyer can see which goods are most successful. She also talks to the department managers to find out how they think sales are going.

Analysing sales figures and deciding what to sell is only part of the buyer's job. The next problem is trying to make sure that everything arrives on the sales floor in the right quantities and at the right times. While some goods may come from a supplier just around the corner, others will have travelled by air and sea from all over the world. Some things, such as a fashionable coat which has suddenly begun to sell better than other designs, may be rushed to the shop straight from the maker's workroom as the buyer and her supplier try to catch the trend at its height. On the other hand, the basic goods like black leather gloves, which the shop would stock regularly, may have to be ordered up to eighteen months in advance. This is because of the need to book long production runs at some factories early on before competing buyers can place their orders. Such goods have what are called long 'lead-times'.

A great deal of time is spent looking for new sources of supply that will enable the store to undersell its competitors or to provide goods of better quality at the same price. This involves much exciting (and exhausting!) travel, during which the buyer will take the opportunity to visit foreign stores and look at competition. She will also visit the yearly international trade fairs, such as the Furniture Fair at Cologne or the Brighton Toy Fair. There, all the firms making these goods exhibit their current and future ranges, from which the buyer will choose new goods for her department.

A week in the life of a furniture buyer

Monday	Tuesday	Wednesday	Thursday	Friday

The buyer works in her office at the department store.	She visits a factory to check the quality of a range.	After discussing sales in the store, she flies to a trade fair.	She talks to a possible supplier about a new line of chairs.	While abroad, she visits a local store to see its goods.

◄ A kitchen furniture buyer checks the mechanism on a folding chair at the Milan Furniture Fair. He may decide to order the chair as it is or ask for changes to meet the needs of his customers.

► Buyers visit factories for several reasons: to study a new process, to check the quality of the raw materials being used or to see whether delivery dates are likely to be met. This factory commune in China produces good quality rattan furniture by traditional methods.

▼ Fashion buyers attend dozens of parades like this every year. Some are given by international fashion houses in Rome, Paris and Milan; others are private viewings in a manufacturer's showroom, where the clothes are modelled by his assistants. Each show will help the buyer to decide which fashion trends to adapt for her customers.

▲ Sometimes a buyer's desk is covered in samples as a succession of suppliers' representatives bring in their latest lines. A toy buyer begins planning for Christmas in January, places some orders in early summer and completes the bulk of them by August.

The buying office

The buying office is the place where what the shop will actually sell is decided. The people who work there are concerned with money and time. They have to keep costs down so that the goods sold by the store are as competitively-priced as possible, and they must ensure that the goods reach the store when they are needed and in the right quantities. A great deal of time is spent on the telephone – chasing missing consignments, inquiring about the reasons for delays, checking on the production of a new item, discussing orders. Everything has to be done promptly, for in buying, tomorrow is always too late.

▲ A carpet buyer discusses a new range of samples with a representative from the manufacturer. Some stores have a carpet warehouse and workrooms as well as space to carry a range of flat carpets in popular colours and patterns.

Buying office clerk

This is often a useful way to enter buying for the clerk has to know everything that the buyer is doing. The job includes maintaining the diary so that appointments do not clash, checking travel arrangements, booking hotels and airline tickets, as well as helping to keep the office running smoothly when the buyer is away.

The clerk must be helpful to suppliers and potential suppliers, and tactful with those whom the buyer is unable or unwilling to see should they arrive without an appointment.

Clerks are also responsible to the buyer and the assistant buyers for checking and processing the orders and deliveries. In many large department store groups buying office clerks are able to call up the necessary information on VDUs (visual display units). These are linked to a central computer which is programmed for stock control. Enquiries can be answered and data amended.

Assistant buyer

The act of buying carries so great a responsibility that few assistant buyers make any major buying decisions. Their main job is to ensure that the orders placed by the buyer are accurate, that the deliveries are made on time and that the goods arrive undamaged and as originally specified.

The assistant buyer runs the office in the buyer's absence. She has to make sure that the stocks of various sizes and colour of goods are kept in balance in the shops which are part of the group. This means that shortages at one shop may have to be made up by moving surplus stock there from another.

Where stock records have not yet been computerized the assistant buyer has to be able to interpret grids, or stock record charts, which are prepared daily by department managers. These show the numbers of goods sold in the department and the numbers that must be re-ordered.

▼ The buyer's secretary has to be helpful, tactful and, above all, efficient, for a buyer's day is largely made up of meeting people.

Department manager/buyer

Where department managers themselves do the buying they have the advantage of knowing how the goods are selling from first-hand experience. They also have full control over the ways in which they are displayed and presented to the customers. However, although a manager/buyer can be particularly sensitive to local preferences, he has to buy in relatively small amounts. He does not, therefore, have the power of a central buyer to negotiate large cost reductions on bulk purchases.

There is no clear-cut route to becoming a manager/buyer other than a thorough grounding in the selling side of retailing, gained through much varied experience.

Central buyer

The central buyer is among the most important, and therefore most highly-paid members of a group of stores. There is no training other than years of practical retailing experience, which must be combined with the necessary flair.

Most buyers for major store groups are graduates. Management skills are as important as a thorough knowledge of the merchandise. A good buyer often moves from one area of selling to another in the course of her career and finds no difficulty in switching from toys to cutlery to perfumery to oriental carpets, for example.

A central buyer for a large group could be responsible for spending more than £5,000,000 a year on goods which must sell fairly quickly in order to remain profitable. Mistakes are very expensive!

There is a large amount of risk involved and the buyer must really know her market. For example, a fabric buyer may need to maintain adequate stocks of more than a thousand different designs and colours. They must be in several branches of the store group at the same time, with deliveries timed six months ahead – not an easy task when wondering in August what the weather will be like in March and whether the government will have made changes to the tax rates which will upset all her calculations!

Some fabric designs may go on selling for over twenty years, and the buyer must ensure that they are always in supply. She must also introduce dozens of new ones each year, only a few of which will last long enough to take their place as winning lines.

In order to take decisions like this she must be able to interpret sales statistics in the light of the reports of customer preferences she receives. She does this by maintaining close and friendly contact with all those who are responsible for selling the goods in the shops.

The buyer must also be able to drive a tough but fair bargain with her suppliers and to take a calculated risk from time to time.

▲ A merchandising director discussing the sales and stock-levels in a department with the merchandiser responsible for controlling them.

▼ Using a visual display unit (VDU) to order goods from a department store group's own central stockrooms. The VDU is linked with a central computer system containing details of stock orders and invoices. The operator can add to or amend the details on the displayed order form by tapping instructions on her keyboard.

◄ Buying offices are not always full of merchandise, but there is enough of it around to remind everyone that they are in the retailing business. The main activities are ordering the goods and making sure that they arrive on time, in the right quantities and at the agreed price.

On display

If you visit a department store's display studio on a hot day in August, you will find that it is already winter! Surrounded by neatly stacked wooden battens and boards, rolls of coloured felt and metallic papers, the designers are busy at their sloping drawing boards. Though they are all wearing summer clothes, one of them is working on a Christmas poster.

One of the display team, wearing a T-shirt, is spraying glitter-frost from a can. He is putting the finishing touches to a Snow Queen's Palace and the two-metre-high mountain of ice upon which it stands. This will form the centrepiece for the toy department throughout November and December.

Beyond it are three full-sized replicas of the store's windows, hung with silver snowflakes. Two display girls are setting up groups of gifts inside the windows.

It all began in March, nine months before Christmas. The display manager and the designers sketched out their initial ideas and discussed them at a series of meetings which involved the store manager and all the merchandise managers.

This year the toy department displays and decorations will have a traditional Christmas theme. The store might have chosen to use characters from a favourite children's book such as *Peter Pan*, from a television series, or from a popular cartoon film. Such displays are often set up with the help of the film or television company concerned and use original props.

Important as they are, the Christmas displays are only a small part of the display department's work throughout the year. Special fashion windows have to be designed for spring and autumn, and each department in turn has a major promotion to display its goods.

The time schedule for each event is worked out six weeks in advance, while display units are built a month before they will be needed. Everything used in the displays has to be ordered or checked in plenty of time. Enormous quantities of basics such as felt, staples and paint are needed to make the floors and backgrounds. All the items in the display have to be selected, collected and booked out of their departments to make sure that every one is accounted for. As well as the actual goods, a vital part of each display is the price tickets and signs. Once designed, these too have to be ordered.

But the display manager does not live in the future all the time. Part of each day is spent walking round all the windows making notes and observations for his team. He is looking for damaged displays, for dust, dirt or wrongly placed tickets. At the same time he judges the effect of each display and points out where, by exchanging one article for another, the colour balance or overall impact might be improved.

◀ Father Christmas, or Santa Claus, is a familiar and timeless figure in many large stores from mid-November to Christmas Eve. Now adapted to the space age, he provides an added attraction in the toy department.

▲ Displays set up inside the store are designed to attract customers to a department. They can be used to bring together matching items, or to hide a staff doorway or service lift.

▼ Together, an assistant and a designer select sweaters for a knitwear window. The best fashion windows have a basic theme, such as a colour or texture. Accessories must also be carefully chosen.

▲ Many shops have angled windows to tempt the viewer further in. Others have no display windows but use their in-store displays, seen through the windows, to attract customers.

Attracting customers

A craftsman kneels on the floor, working frantically with fibreglass and paint as displays are put up around him. He is mending the hull of a prototype sailing dinghy, which was damaged when it arrived from the manufacturer. It will form the centre-piece of an Outdoor Living exhibition held to attract customers thinking about their summer holidays at home and abroad.

The damaged boat is a final, temporary hitch, after three months of discussions and planning which involved the managers of merchandise, display, public relations, advertising, five different buyers and several of their suppliers. At their meetings they discussed every aspect. How much will the exhibition cost? £800? £1,500? Will it stimulate enough sales and bring more customers to the shop? How much of the cost can be absorbed by existing advertising and display budgets? Will the suppliers contribute financially? Should leaflets be mailed with customer accounts? Because it is a prototype, the dinghy is newsworthy. How should the press be brought in? Should a celebrity be invited to the opening? How much would he cost? Could the space be better used to sell goods? These are just a few of the questions which have to be answered by the people involved in planning an exhibition of this type.

Some department stores are large enough to have an exhibition area which can be used for different kinds of promotion, from fashion shows and demonstrations of products to art exhibitions and other events intended to attract customers rather than to sell the goods in the exhibition. Many department stores encourage suppliers to stage promotions for their own products within the shop. Some, on the other hand, are against this, feeling that the shop's overall image is more important.

Advertising policies are just as varied and often change from year to year. Britain's largest group of stores recently spent over £1,000,000 on one year's advertising; the second largest spent more than £3,000,000 and the third largest less than £6,000.

The form of advertising also varies. Many stores now buy time on local radio as well as space in newspapers, using catchy jingles to make their names memorable. Television advertising has a far wider audience but is also far more expensive.

Promotions and advertising have been called 'extensions of the shop window'. Like it, they are intended to catch and hold the customer's attention, persuading him to buy one item rather than another and in this store rather than that one.

The store's long-term links with the community are handled by its public relations staff. They are responsible for making sure that the store has good relations with its suppliers, the local authorities, the police, other traders, the press, and a wide range of powerful groups and local organisations.

However effective a shop's advertising and promotions may be, a well-earned reputation for high standards, fair dealing and good relationships with staff and customers is still its greatest asset.

► A press officer telephones the features editor of a do-it-yourself magazine with a suggestion for an article. Large stores keep in close contact with those on newspapers and magazines who produce fashion and homemaking features. Coats and dresses, candles and cushions, fabrics and furniture are all sent on loan to editorial offices so that rooms can be set up and photographed. In return, the store is credited in the caption to the photograph.

▲ Free sampling is a long-established way of introducing customers to new products. Food halls often have special weeks devoted to the produce of one country. Above, English teas are being tasted, while on the right, girls in traditional costume offer samples of Dutch cheese.

◄ Many customers are attracted by the chance to see a famous personality and perhaps get their autograph. This author is signing copies of his best-selling novel. The customers will probably buy something else in the shop before they leave.

► Beauty consultants teach customers how to use new make-up techniques. There is no charge for this service apart from the cost of the cosmetics if the customer decides to buy them.

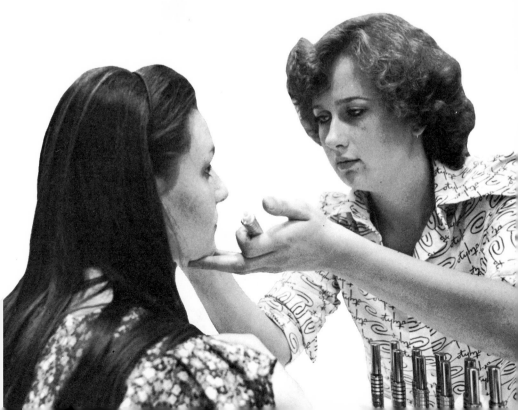

The image makers

An essential part of selling is presenting the goods as attractively as possible. This includes not only the arrangement of the shop windows and display stands, but also the appearance of the sales team, the way in which the store is decorated and its overall image. In all these, the people who work in design, display and public relations play a vital part. Their contribution to the success of the store is in many ways as important as that made by those who meet the customer on the sales floor.

Window display

Display staff are recruited direct from schools, art schools and colleges. Physical fitness is as vital as artistic ability because it is often necessary to lift and carry fairly heavy display boards and other equipment.

Juniors usually start as helpers to a senior window-dresser. Their progress then depends on their ability and flair. Some work best with dress fabrics, creating fashions on window models by pinning and draping lengths of material. Others may be good at arranging objects like glassware and kitchen gadgets into exciting groupings or pinning scarves and gloves to felt-covered boards for interior displays.

Most department store display teams start work before the store opens and leave before it closes. A few members are left on 'bell call' in case last-minute adjustments are needed, for example, if an item has been sold from a window display.

Display managers are promoted from within the store or recruited after several years of window display experience in other shops.

Design adviser

Store groups employ a design adviser who is responsible for the visual appearance or 'house-style' of the group. This includes the kind of type-face in which the store name must always appear, the colour and lettering of the sales tickets, letterheads and other stationery, the interior design of the stores themselves, the staff uniforms and the livery of the delivery vans.

The design adviser is consulted on the basic appearance of the store's advertising, whenever a major change is made to a department or store layout and when any work that alters the exterior appearance is planned. This job is unlikely to be open to anybody who has not had many years of experience in a major area of design since leaving art school.

▲ Felt, board and quick-drying emulsion paint are the most frequently used materials in window displays. Staple guns are used to fix the felt to panels, which then form the backing boards or bases for displays.

◄ Modern window-models are lifelike but very expensive, so must be handled and stored carefully. Here a group for a sportswear display is being assembled. Artistic judgement is needed if the finished pose is to look natural.

Advertising manager

Advertising, promotions, press and publicity are handled in a variety of ways by different department stores and store groups. These activities often overlap. Sometimes they are the responsibility of the advertising department, sometimes of the press and public relations officer.

A department store in a small town probably has its own advertising manager and an assistant. Together, they devise the advertising campaigns in the local press. Many stores now also produce commercials which are relayed by local radio stations.

Department store groups with enough shops in most parts of the country may use advertisements in the national press to keep the group's name in the public mind. They will probably appoint a major advertising agency to handle their account.

This means that the agency is responsible for all the group's advertising, which will be produced by a 'creative team', made up from the agency's specialised personnel. This will include a typographic designer, a copywriter and a media specialist, who would advise on the choices between newspapers, magazines, local radio and television best suited to the needs of the 'client'—in this case, the department store group. The team will also include an 'account executive'. His job is to work closely with the store group's advertising manager on all aspects of the advertising campaigns.

Many advertisements in group campaigns are wholly or partly paid for by suppliers of fashions, china and glass, electrical goods, audio equipment and other merchandise for which the department store is named as a major stockist.

Catalogues and informative leaflets for customers are also produced by the advertising or promotions department or, sometimes, by its advertising agency.

An advertising manager for a store which does not use an agency will be involved in booking photographers, arranging for merchandise to be sent to studios, and in working with the display department on room settings for furniture and fashion shots.

He also has to be an expert on printing processes, able to call on specialist printers for anything from a glossy showcard or Christmas restaurant menu to a full colour brochure announcing a Finnish furniture week.

► 'Fine . . . now hold it . . . Good . . . chin up a little . . . hold it . . . great ! . .' A photographer will take endless shots of one pose to make sure of getting exactly the right one for a catalogue or advertisement.

▲ Store interiors are always changing, as departments contract or expand to make way for new sales or display areas. The designs and plans are usually produced in the store's own design studio.

Press and public relations

The press office deals with newspaper inquiries concerning retailing. It also helps journalists writing home-making and fashion features by supplying information about new merchandise, lending samples for photography, and helping to devise room settings for magazine photographic features. It organizes press shows from time to time to launch new fashion or fabric collections. It may also help suppliers to stage exhibitions of glassware and other products in the shop.

A group press and public relations officer advises management on overall public relations policies. He or she is likely to have spent many years in journalism, public relations or advertising.

▼ A rather unusual idea of window-dressing !

Press officer

There may be a group press officer and a press officer/advertising manager at individual shops within the group. These will be experienced people but both will head a team of assistants, some of whom will be in their first jobs.

Press and merchandise assistants

These are responsible for various aspects of work in a press office, including the collation and circulation of press clippings, production of press releases, printing of brochures and leaflets and general inquiries from outside organizations.

Merchandise assistants help journalists to prepare merchandise features and articles. They are recruited from schools, universities or specialist colleges.

Customer care

When you walk into a department store you may be tired or cheerful, rushing to buy something before the shops shut or out enjoying a spending spree. Whoever you are and however you feel, *you* are the customer. You must be made welcome and every effort made to help you to shop successfully and in comfort, The reasons are obvious – if shopping in a particular store is easy and enjoyable, the customer will buy more and come back again.

Everything possible is done to help you find what you are looking for. As well as clearly displayed signs there is an information desk, staffed by friendly and helpful people. They can tell you where to find cassette tapes, or the dressmaking adviser, or a place where babies can be fed in privacy.

If the hairdrier you buy turns out to be faulty, the store will replace it or refund the money. If your problem or complaint is more complicated, a specialist from the customer service or goodwill department will help to find an answer that is fair to everyone. Some stores have roof gardens, where tired shoppers can get a breath of country air in the centre of the city. Lifts and escalators, wash-rooms and nursery rooms where mothers can look after their babies are all intended to encourage people to spend long periods in the shop. The most modern department stores have multi-storey or underground car parks from which the customer can reach the sales floors under cover, thus avoiding the street and its rival attractions altogether!

Behind the sales departments is a wide range of back-up services: hire purchase and credit accounts, workrooms where curtains and upholstery are made up from fabrics bought in the store, carpet fitters who lay wall-to-wall floor coverings in the customer's home, and a design service for kitchens and bathrooms, the cost of which is refunded if the customer buys the units suggested. Most stores have hairdressing salons and manicure parlours; some have a wedding present service which holds a list of the gifts requested by the bride from which the givers can select. Others will arrange an entire wedding, from booking cars to arranging catering and photography.

The biggest stores have banks, estate agents, food halls and a claim to be able to obtain anything a customer might want, from a rare antique to a camel – at a price!

Department stores try to make shopping enjoyable as well as easy. Most have one or more places to eat – often an inexpensive quick-service counter for shoppers in a hurry and a restaurant with table service and a high quality menu for those who regard a relaxing meal with a friend as the highlight of a day's shopping.

▼ 'Suede by the metre? Through the arch and to your right. Coffee bar? Fourth floor. Gas stoves? Escalator to the basement and turn left. . . .' The staff on the information desk deal with hundreds of such queries every day, as well as with such curiosities as 'Do you sell twelve-year-old shirts?'

▲ Some lifts are operated by the customers themselves but a helpful lift attendant can make shopping much easier.

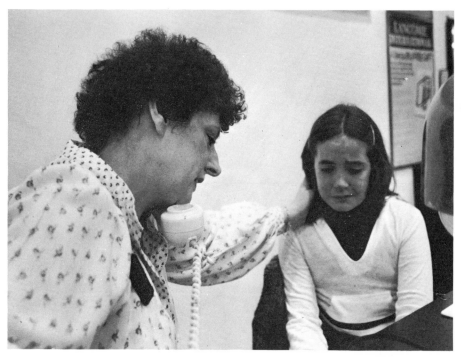

▼ Curtains which have been made for a customer are checked for length and pattern match before dispatch. Small weights sewn into the lower hem make sure that the curtains hang straight, and a steam comb is used to set the pleating.

▲ Losing mother in a large crowd is very upsetting. 'Never mind, dear. I'll just call the telephone lady and then we'll count the seconds until we hear her telling your mother where you are. She'll soon be here . . . '

▼ Hairstyles are as much a part of fashion as clothes. A visit to the hairdressing salon, whether unisex or more traditional, often forms part of a day's shopping. Some stores also offer an ear-piercing service.

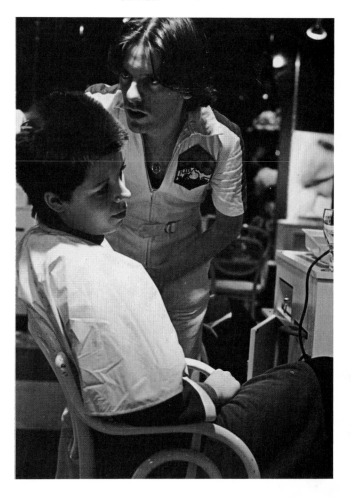

Bargains galore

Everybody loves a bargain. Twice a year – in early summer and immediately after the Christmas rush – department stores erupt in signs which shout 'Drastic Reductions!' or 'Prices Slashed!'

Sales are held primarily to clear slow-moving or out-of-date goods, so freeing money and space for the new season's stock. The manufacturer also uses them to clear stock, which is offered to department store buyers at lower than normal rates. These 'special purchases' often include hundreds of manufacturer's 'seconds', particularly in china and glass. These are normal quality goods which have minor flaws such as a blurred design or a bubble in the glass, which means they cannot be sold as 'perfect'. Others, while 'perfect', are from broken or discontinued ranges. They are usually sold at half to one third less than the usual selling price.

Fashion departments are also happy hunting grounds for bargain seekers. A mild winter brings huge reductions in winter coat prices as the buyers try to clear space for the spring purchases. In a cold spring people put off buying lighter weight clothing, which then has to be reduced in the summer sale.

Many people save all year for a spending spree at the sales. The biggest department store in London expects sales of at least £3,000,000 from just the first day! Queues form very early in the morning and people sometimes camp on the pavement for several days and nights before the sale. To encourage this – and the resultant publicity – some stores put several expensive goods with extreme price reductions in their windows up to a week before the sale. They then issue priority

▲ The sales queue outside a major London department store on the first day of its summer sale. Some early arrivals will have been camping on the pavement for several days and nights to be sure of the pick of the bargains.

tickets to the first people to start a queue. Other stores consider that a customer should be able to buy anything displayed for sale and so do not offer 'one-off' bargains of that kind.

This twice-yearly 'sales fever', as it is often called, is unknown in some countries. There, stores offer bargains throughout the year. However, where sales are common they are likely to continue, for manufacturer, supplier and shop all work to this twice-yearly pattern.

Typical yearly sales. Notice where the highest and lowest sales occur. Why is this?

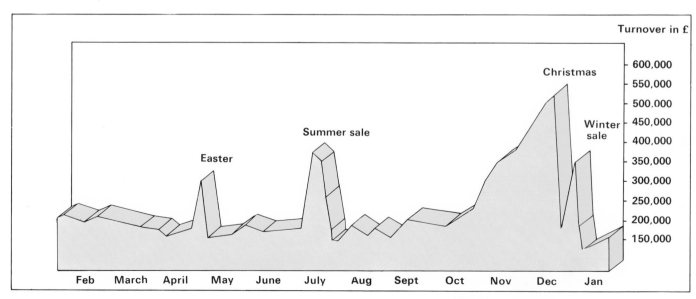

Turnover in £

Christmas

Winter sale

Summer sale

Easter

600,000
550,000
500,000
450,000
400,000
350,000
300,000
250,000
200,000
150,000

Feb · March · April · May · June · July · Aug · Sept · Oct · Nov · Dec · Jan

▲ Opening the doors on the first day of a sale. Bargain hunters race through the shop and up the escalators to secure the pick of the reduced goods in their favourite departments. It can be dangerous to fall down!

▼ China and glass 'seconds' at between half and a third less than normal price are among the most popular buys at sale time.

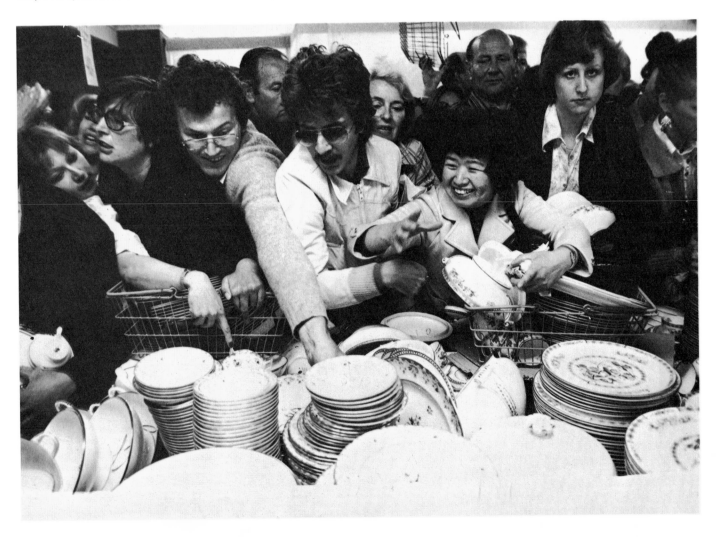

'Come with me, please'

▲ 'Excuse me, madam, but have you paid for all of those coats?'

▼ Fur, suede and leather coats are favourite targets for shoplifters. The coats on this rail are being linked together by chains through the sleeves. These can be unlocked by an assistant if a customer wants to try a coat on.

It begins quietly enough. The security office receives a call from the men's wear department: two customers – a man and a woman – are having a noisy argument near the cash point.

'Thank you. We'll keep an eye on it.' Immediately, a store detective in her outdoor clothes takes a short cut down the staff staircase and becomes engrossed in looking at a rack of sheepskin coats. She notes that the arguing couple have now involved two assistants and a section manager. The woman is getting hysterical but the detective is not watching her. Her attention is fixed closely on the dozen or so other customers who are reacting to the incident with varying degrees of amusement or irritation.

Suddenly the argument subsides and the woman marches out. The man shrugs and follows her. The department manager approaches the store detective as if she were a customer but says quietly, 'Chap in dark overcoat . . . couple of suits under it. Saw him in the mirror. . .'

It was, as had been suspected, two professional shoplifters creating a diversion so that another thief could operate relatively unobserved. The store detective now has to keep the thief under observation to make sure that he does not pass the stolen goods to an accomplice unnoticed before he can be challenged upon leaving the shop.

Shoplifting can be a major problem for a department store without an efficient security system. Some rely almost entirely on store detectives; others also use a variety of surveillance devices, not all of which are apparent to the customers. These include one-way mirrors, curved mirrors and cameras relaying information to the screens in the security office.

Shoplifters are usually prosecuted, and fines can be enormous. The store detective's polite questioning and subsequent request: 'Will you come with me, please...' can be a costly experience.

Shoplifting is only one way in which a store may incur 'wastage'. This covers all losses, both known and unaccounted for, from simple human errors such as cutting fabric the wrong length to serious dishonesties like pilfering. The security force keeps a wary eye on any area where dishonesty may occur, such as the cashpoints. It is also responsible for the overall security of the store and has to check all window and door locks.

Catching shoplifters is dramatic and highly publicised. But it is only part of the story.

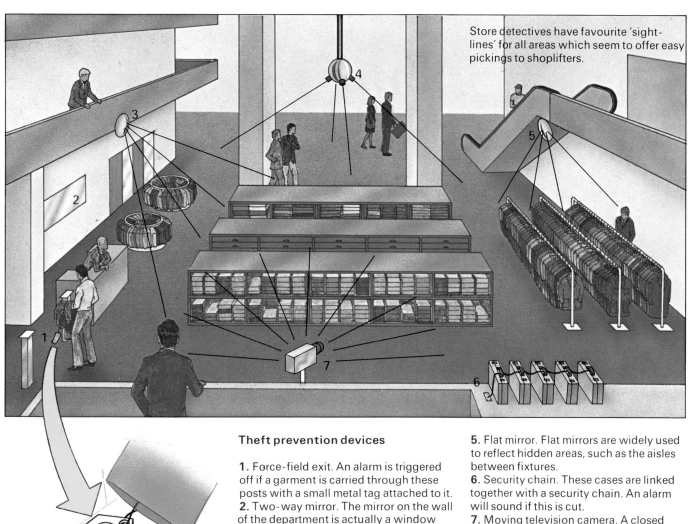

Store detectives have favourite 'sight-lines' for all areas which seem to offer easy pickings to shoplifters.

Theft prevention devices

1. Force-field exit. An alarm is triggered off if a garment is carried through these posts with a small metal tag attached to it.

2. Two-way mirror. The mirror on the wall of the department is actually a window from the department manager's office.

3. Parabolic mirror. Convex mirrors give a wide, if distorted view of the department for staff and store detectives.

4. Multi-lens television camera. The multi-lens, multi-directional television scanner revolves or sweeps.

5. Flat mirror. Flat mirrors are widely used to reflect hidden areas, such as the aisles between fixtures.

6. Security chain. These cases are linked together with a security chain. An alarm will sound if this is cut.

7. Moving television camera. A closed circuit television scanner sweeps from side to side, and up and down. The most advanced types are fitted with zoom lenses and can be controlled from the security office to give general or close-up views. They can also be linked to a video-tape recorder for action replays.

▲ In most department stores, items of clothing such as shirts, dresses, coats and trousers have tags attached. These are either magnetic or electronic, and are removed by the assistant when the goods are paid for.

► Small items of silverware are all too easily slipped into bags or pockets, so are usually displayed behind glass. If they are on open display they are wired together. An alarm sounds if the wires are cut.

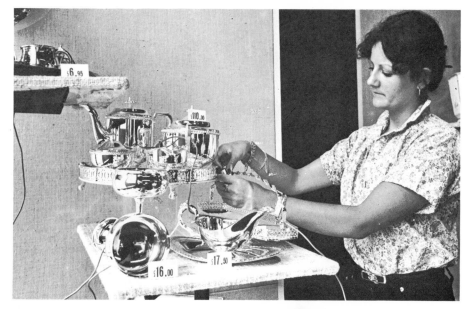

Emergency!

The voice booming from the loudspeakers throughout the store is calm and matter-of-fact. But its message is urgent. 'This is the managing director speaking. We have an emergency which requires the evacuation of the building. Please proceed to the nearest exit as directed by our staff. . .' The fire wardens responsible for each area pick up red electric torches and move into action. It is their responsibility to ensure that nobody is left behind.

All members of the sales staff know the nearest exits – and alternative exit routes – from their departments. It is their job to guide customers out, assuring them if necessary that they are in a modern building which is well provided with exits, all round and on all floors.

The staff handbook instructs them to 'keep a special look-out for small children, the elderly and infirm and give assistance wherever possible. Do not run, but walk at a smart pace!'

Outside the shop several check points have been set up, each with lists of specific areas for which the fire wardens are responsible. One by one the fire wardens report 'Everyone clear' and their area numbers are marked off. Less than seven minutes after the managing director's voice was first heard the store has been completely cleared. Without customers, this evacuation can take less than three minutes!

On this occasion there was no emergency. It was a full-scale version of the staff drills performed several times a year, and which form the basic routine for dealing with any emergency. Some customers grumble at their shopping being disturbed; others are more appreciative of the calm efficiency and speed with which the staff cleared the store.

By the time the store was empty, a real fire would have been sealed off from the rest of the building by heavy metal shutters. Behind them the heat would have activated sprinklers in the ceiling, releasing a deluge of water. All the staff are trained in the use of fire-fighting equipment, such as extinguishers and hoses, which is checked regularly.

Safety is very important in a department store. The escalators have finely-grooved steps and grills, in which it is almost impossible to trap your feet or fingers. Should you manage to do so, an electronic device will stop the mechanism immediately. Lift doors will not close if an electronic beam at child and pushchair level is interrupted. If they do close gently on something, their sprung edges activate a switch which will open them again.

Finally, if, despite all precautions, a customer injures herself or is taken ill, trained nurses from the staff medical room are on hand to give instant attention.

▲ Fire could spread with frightening speed in a poorly protected department store if the initial outbreak is not detected and dealt with promptly. Staff are trained to use extinguishers but the greatest protection comes from overhead sprinklers.

▼ Fire hoses are placed so that no part of the shop is beyond the reach of one or more jets of water. This wall-pivoted hose is being pulled out for inspection, and its stopcock is being checked.

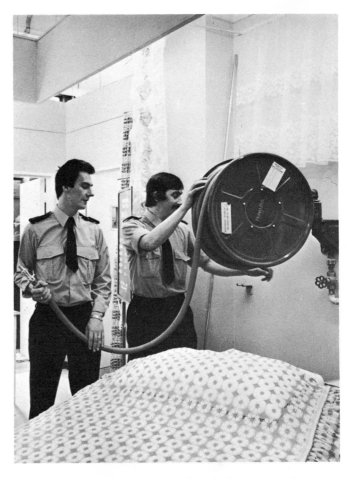

▶ Department stores are full of safety devices, some of which are shown here.

► She may just have fainted — perhaps she rushed to the sales without breakfast and forgot to stop for lunch. But it may be serious. A trained nurse from the medical room decides whether a doctor or an ambulance should be called.

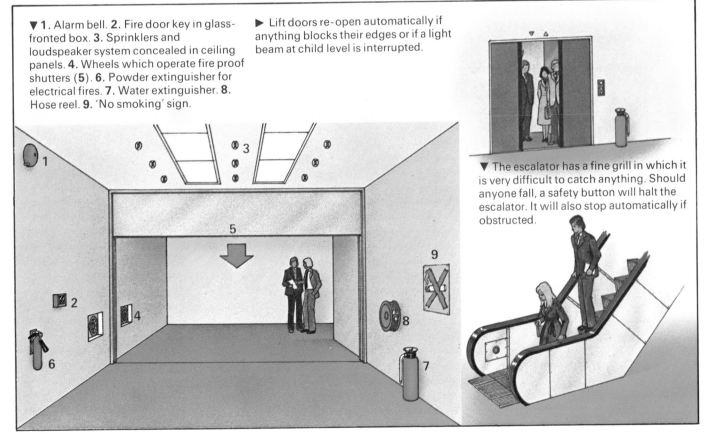

▼ 1. Alarm bell. 2. Fire door key in glass-fronted box. 3. Sprinklers and loudspeaker system concealed in ceiling panels. 4. Wheels which operate fire proof shutters (5). 6. Powder extinguisher for electrical fires. 7. Water extinguisher. 8. Hose reel. 9. 'No smoking' sign.

► Lift doors re-open automatically if anything blocks their edges or if a light beam at child level is interrupted.

▼ The escalator has a fine grill in which it is very difficult to catch anything. Should anyone fall, a safety button will halt the escalator. It will also stop automatically if obstructed.

Behind the scenes

Like painting a huge bridge, maintaining a large department store is a never-ending process. Every day more than 2500 square metres of display windows have to be cleaned. Over 3000 fluorescent tubes and light bulbs have to be checked and replaced. Tonnes of rubbish have to be moved out. There are display units to be built, doors to be rehung, broken furniture to be mended, torn carpeting to be replaced. . . . And each night it must all be locked up, checked and patrolled to make sure that it remains secure.

▲ An electrician checks the control box wiring for one of the motors powering the air conditioning system. Two more electricians are stripping another motor to clean the brushes and commutator.

▶ Cooks and other kitchen staff are an essential part of a department store. They provide food for the store's employees as well as for its customers.

◀ Planing a wooden batten for a display stand. Carpentry is an important skill in a department store: storage shelves and cupboards have to be made up and fitted, and there are always repairs to desks, counters, windows and doors to be carried out.

Maintenance

This is the responsibility of the service manager. It is his team of tradesmen and craftsmen, engineers, plumbers, carpenters and electricians who keep the shop presentable and fully operational.

Electricians

The house electrician and his team carry out regular inspections of the wiring concealed behind ceilings and within pillars and skirting boards, and make sure that the motors working the air conditioning have a weekly check.

They install extra lighting points where needed. Spotlights last only three weeks; the fire alarms are checked daily and the sprinkler system once a week. There is

also a standby generator to be maintained in case of power cuts. One or more of the electricians must be prepared to be called out at night to attend to an emergency, such as a faulty burglar alarm.

Electricians serve an apprenticeship and can be fully qualified by the age of 21. The team will include one or more young apprentices who are learning the theoretical aspects on paid day release.

Plumbers

These have two main areas of responsibility — the washrooms for staff and customers and the automatic sprinkler system which covers the ceilings with its network of nozzles throughout the building. They too, have served apprenticeships.

Carpenters

Most carpenters specialize in shopfitting — building shelves, cupboards, etc. — and in making fitments for window displays. A few concentrate on the maintenance of offices, stockrooms and their furniture. They are qualified tradesmen, often with experience in building work, who have served apprenticeships.

Painters

The painter and his team work steadily throughout the year. Their time is divided between routine jobs, like repainting the rest rooms and offices on a rota, and meeting irregular demands, such as redecorating an area for a new selling department.

Cleaning

All the selling floors have to be swept and polished and the carpets vacuumed before the shop opens each day. A large store will have fifty or more cleaners working in two shifts. They pay particular attention to areas such as the entrances, where thousands of pairs of feet carry in layer upon layer of dirt and dust. The exterior display windows are also cleaned daily.

Huge quantities of rubbish — paper and cardboard cartons, plastics and discarded display aids from the shop; paper and hundreds of metres of computer print-out sheets from the offices — are removed daily. Some of it is bagged up and goes down a chute to a basement incinerator; some is compacted in a crushing machine and sent for recycling and the rest is put into a skip and taken away by the local authority refuse disposal service.

▲ The telephonist is often a customer's first contact with a store. Her voice and manner help to decide whether the customer shops there or goes elsewhere. Every day each telephonist probably deals with more than a thousand calls.

▼ Department stores contain a great deal of metal, used in shelves, display units, trolleys and racks. Smaller stores may call in outside help when repairs are needed, but much expense can be saved if a store has a well-equipped workshop. Here the broken underframe of a trolley used for moving goods to and from the stockrooms is being welded.

Deliveries

Delivery men are an important link between the shop and its customers. Cheerfulness and resourcefulness are qualifications almost as important as the ability to handle large vans. Sometimes a customer forgets to mention that a sofa will need to be carried up a flight of narrow stairs and manoeuvred over the banisters; others will have omitted to tie up the dog!

Security

The security team in a large department store will include about eight store detectives and fifteen uniformed men who supervise staff exits, ensure that keys are taken by authorized people, signed for and returned. They also carry out security checks and searches and, from time to time, assist a store detective in making an arrest.

Store detectives

These do not necessarily have experience of police work, but they usually work under a chief security officer who has already completed a successful career in the police force. Some are sales staff who have shown an aptitude for spotting and coping with shoplifters. Physical fitness, intelligence, a good memory and impeccable character references are essential qualifications for security work. Store detectives are trained in self-defence, the law relating to powers of arrest and the giving of evidence in court where much of a store detective's time is spent. It is also necessary to be able to write clear, concise reports.

The security officer and his team are also concerned from time to time with the internal auditor whose job includes checking — and often devising — security systems to prevent fraud through the misuse of till procedures, computer systems, invoices and other paper work.

Cash and credit

▲ The operator of this visual display unit (VDU) uses it to inspect all the orders and invoices controlling the receipt and delivery of goods.

Once, not long ago, shops were noisy with the ringing and banging of cash registers as their keys were pressed, the fingers bobbed up and the drawers shot out. Today's tills have electronic brains and are almost silent. They represent a new technology which is being applied to the gathering of sales information and the control of stock in the store.

But the dialogue on the sales floor has hardly changed.

'Cash or account, Madam?'·

'Account, please. Here is my card. I would like the goods delivered.' This customer has a monthly account and has arranged to pay for all purchases at the end of each month. If she had paid cash and taken the goods with her the till would have produced a receipt slip for her. As the goods are to be delivered and charged to her account the details are recorded on a carbon-backed three-part bill which is inserted into the till. This provides a record for the selling department, a receipt for the customer and delivery instructions to the dispatch department.

Even when such bills have to be written out by hand they include a simple code which can be used by the accounts department to identify the kind of goods being sold. The electronic tills now used in most big department stores do much more than that. A code of only seven figures can be used to identify the selling department concerned, the article being sold (e.g. tennis racket) and the particular model. Besides doing all this the till's illuminated digital display tells both the sales assistant and the customer the price, the amount of cash handed over and the change to be given back.

There is, however, a limit to the amount of coded information about the type, colour and size of article which a sales assistant can be expected to tap out on a keyboard. In the newest tills, thirty or more separate pieces of information about each sale are recorded

literally at the wave of a wand! Each price ticket is magnetically marked with a code containing all the information. The sales assistant passes the tip of a small metal wand across this number, which is then automatically transferred to the bill.

In the most advanced systems the codes pass directly into the store group's central computer. This analyses the data and prints it out in the various forms required by buyers, financial advisers and store managers. Some computers are even able to take over such detailed and laborious tasks as re-ordering goods from the warehouse as soon as stocks in the shop fall to a certain level!

A typical accounts system

The **accountant** advises the **store manager** on the shop's finances – whether it can afford to expand, the profit it must make to pay all its bills, and so on. The **deputy accountant** runs the **expenses office.** This deals with the costs of running the business, including paying suppliers for the goods stocked in the shop. It also produces the Trading (or profit and loss) Account. The **cash office** collects the day's takings and banks them. It provides cash for the **pay office** to make up the wage packets. **Dissections** analyses the goods sold into groups to guide the buyers and provides the statistics upon which future buying budgets are based. **Costing and invoicing** checks suppliers' bills against goods received and keeps a running record of goods in stock. **Sales and accounts** supervises customer accounts for the **credit manager,** who is responsible for promoting the shop's hire purchase, budget accounts and other credit facilities.

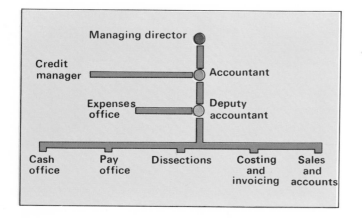

▲ The development of electronic calculators has revolutionized accounting procedures, speeding them up enormously and removing much of the potential for human error.

▲ Every purchase is recorded in the sales ledger. Electric machines with special keyboards and extra-wide carriages to take the large pages are used for this. In fully-computerized systems the figures are fed directly into a computer.

► Vertical files like these carry several hundred names and addresses of customers or suppliers for quick and easy reference. Each is on a thin strip of card which can be removed and altered if necessary.

▼ The three-part bill

This is the basis for all sales in departments without computer-linked tills. Each leaf is printed a different colour for easy identification. The top and middle leaves are carbon-backed so that the details written by the assistant on the top copy are transferred to the other two.

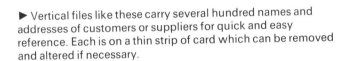

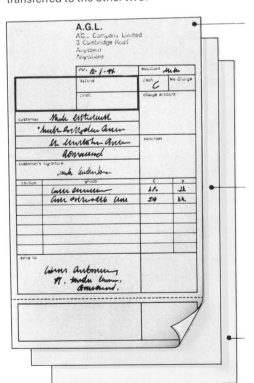

Top copy: goes to the accounts department which checks serial numbers to make sure that all bills are accounted for and that the bill has either been paid or charged to the customer's account. The department also records the details for the trading account and stock control.

Middle copy: goes to the customer if she is taking the goods with her. If they are to be delivered she is given the counterfoil as proof of purchase. The rest of the bill goes to the dispatch department as an authority for the goods to leave the shop.

Bottom copy: is kept by the department as a check on sales and who made them, and in case of a subsequent query or complaint.

▼ The computer till

Many stores have installed advanced computer tills like this one. The metal-tipped 'wand' on the right is passed across the magnetic code printed on each price ticket. It records the details contained in the code and relays them to the store's central computer. The price is shown on the upper digital display screen while the lower one gives instructions to the operator. The bill is inserted on the left and details such as price and method of payment are recorded on it.

The packing experts

When a customer buys a fragile glass bowl and takes it with him it is his responsibility to get it home safely. The assistant will have wrapped it carefully in layers of strong tissue paper, but if the customer drops the bowl he has only himself to blame. However, if he has asked the store to deliver it he will expect it to arrive undamaged. Before it reaches the customer, his bowl will have been carried or wheeled several hundred metres through shop and warehouse, loaded and unloaded, and driven about in vans. Careful packing and handling at every stage is therefore vital.

Many goods remain in the carefully designed packs provided by the manufacturer. Articles such as record decks are usually cocooned in moulded plastic or expanded polystyrene inside their boxes. Dresses travel in plastic bags to keep them clean. The corners of tables and chairs are protected by pieces of strong card or plastic. The legs are wrapped in paper strips and the whole piece is then covered in polythene sheeting.

But what about the glassware, the lampshades and other easily broken or dented items sold from the displays in the shop? This is where the packing experts come in. Each department selling easily damaged items has its own stockroom and specialist packers. They work at tables surrounded by flattened cardboard boxes of various sizes in which goods can be packed, and with a variety of loose fillings that can be pushed into cavities and empty corners. These range from straw and torn-up newspapers to polythene beads and, more recently, computer print-out paper shredded into strips in an electrically operated machine. Lampshades, mirrors and framed pictures are wrapped in transparent plastic full of shock-absorbing bubbles.

All this is happening in the stockrooms, the vast area which is never seen by the customer. Access to them is through heavy, spring-loaded double doors or narrow gaps behind displays, always guarded by large signs proclaiming STAFF ONLY. Downstairs the sub-basement is bustling with activity as goods are wheeled in and out, checked, wrapped and labelled.

Behind one of the steel mesh partitions which divide the stockrooms a rocking horse is being wrapped. Soon it will be wheeled into the link van which will take it from the store to the warehouse, where it will be transferred to a delivery van. The customer, the salesgirl, the stockkeeper, the packers and the four people concerned with the dispatch and delivery of the rocking horse are all making sure that it will arrive unexpectedly as well as safely, for its docket states – 'Deliver to 37, NOT to above address'. Somewhere a child is going to have a wonderful birthday surprise!

▲ Whenever goods are being loaded or unloaded, each item is re-checked against a list called a way-bill. This is done at every point from the time it leaves the department in the shop to when it reaches the customer's home. This means that it should be possible to find any item at any stage of its journey.

▼ Each piece of china in a tea or dinner service has to be individually wrapped to avoid chipping.

▲ A delivery manager and a driver discuss whether an urgent parcel can be included. The driver decides the sequence in which the parcels are delivered and loads the van accordingly, taking into account such things as peak traffic times.

▶ Parcels and packages may be light but awkward or small but heavy. Delivery men are always welcome and enjoy the variety of their work. Like the sales assistants, they carry the shop's reputation with them.

▼ One of a line of parcel wrapping stations in the post orders department. The finished parcel is labelled, weighed, franked and put into a wheeled bin for collection and dispatch by post.

▼ Carefully wrapped chairs awaiting dispatch in a stockroom.

Running the store

A successful department store depends on good management at every level of its complex financial, administrative and selling operations. The most junior employee must feel that he is able to make a real contribution to these. He must be involved and interested, actively enjoying his part in the huge team needed to keep the store running smoothly and profitably. Making sure, that he, and everyone else, feels this is one of the managers' most important functions.

▲ Interviews for jobs or promotion are important stages in everyone's career. A good interviewer can make all the difference.

Store manager

For about four hours every day, usually in the morning, the store manager cannot be found in his office. This is the time he spends visiting all parts of his shop, from sales floor to vanyard. It is called the 'floor walk', and is a major part of his job.

He is there to see and be seen, to discuss plans and problems with managers and assistant managers, to get to know new members of staff by sight, to stimulate people at all levels to think about their working areas and how they might be improved. He will be watching customers and trying to get the feel of the day's trade.

Above all, are the shop and its staff looking brisk, efficient and welcoming? If they are it probably means that one of the most important management responsibilities – that of the welfare and well-being of staff – is in good hands.

Personnel

A good and happy relationship between staff and customers is essential to successful retailing. The personnel department is responsible for the welfare of the people it recruits as well as for their training and development.

It has to take account of the higher numbers of sales staff needed to cope with the Christmas rush and the summer sale. These are usually temporary staff, such as students and housewives, who often work there year after year. The store manager and his advisers assess the staff levels that will be required to meet their estimated forecasts of trade for each month of the year. This is very difficult, and can be expensive if the wrong figure is reached. Overstaffing means higher costs and less profit; understaffing means lost sales and less profit.

The personnel department maintains contact with local employment offices, schools and other sources for recruitment. It advertises vacancies as they occur and advises department managers on the people they choose – usually by interviewing applicants first and picking three or four for a short list to be seen by the department manager. Members of the personnel department – usually the team of interviewers – visit local schools frequently and organize evening events at which young people and their parents can discuss career prospects.

The *staff trainer* arranges induction courses for new recruits as well as further training to management level, both inside the company and through outside colleges and training centres. The personnel department may also include a reference library from which training books and film strips may be borrowed.

The personnel department keeps staff records and statistics, and establishes the wages and salary structure. It therefore needs to keep a close eye on rates paid by competitors.

It also has a general responsibility for ensuring compliance with government acts laying down health and safety requirements. These may include medical services, hygiene in canteens and kitchens, rest rooms with comfortable furnishings and a safety committee concerned with fire and accident prevention throughout the store.

▼ A manager usually writes and answers correspondence first thing every morning. His secretary types his letters and internal memoranda while he attends meetings and deals with the rest of his work. The letters are then ready for him to sign in time to catch the afternoon post.

Medical care

A staff medical room with one or more nursing sisters on daily duty, and often with access to a Company doctor as well as to a local general practitioner, is now a normal part of a big store's welfare service. Several stores also have visiting chiropodists! One London-based stores group has a fully equipped physiotherapy room with a qualified physiotherapist in attendance for the treatment of minor sprains and other muscular problems.

Welfare officer

The welfare officer is someone to whom people can take personal and domestic problems as well as any difficulties over work or promotion. Social and sporting facilities, clubs and societies within the store and sometimes a house magazine are often set up and supervised by the welfare officer.

Catering

Good facilities for meals and for tea and coffee breaks are particularly necessary for shop staff, most of whom are on their feet throughout the working day.

▲ The staff canteen is somewhere to relax and meet friends in the middle of the working day. Meals are subsidized and the management is aware of the importance of good quality food served in pleasant surroundings.

▼ Once a week the shop opens half an hour later than normal so that each department can have a communications session with its manager. This is used for staff announcements, training, discussion of new selling systems and other developments affecting the department.

▼ After standing behind a counter all day a pedicure is extremely welcome!

In the future the customer will be able to shop without leaving her home. By pressing buttons, different articles can be viewed on a three-dimensional television screen. The price and order number are shown and the customer can order the item by pressing this number and that of her own credit card.

In the future

The great dome high above is pierced with multi-coloured patterns. Below it rise tier upon tier of shops, half-seen through the shimmering spray of a fountain which dominates the open central area where shoppers stroll or hurry.

No, not the future but one of the hundreds of new shopping centres which are being built today all over the world. The big department stores with 'everything under one roof' are changing. Some are part of huge indoor complexes of different shops. Others are vast vertical structures, like one fourteen-storey department store in Tokyo. Elsewhere, as in Canada, the winter cold has driven shops underground where they are linked with hotels and carparks.

The technology of retailing is also changing fast. The next ten years will be the decade of the microprocessor. Entire computer systems will be contained on a single microscopic silica chip. This means that the shopkeeper will have instant access to unlimited information on stock levels and sales figures, while the customer will be able to inspect a vast selection of goods on a three-dimensional television screen in the comfort and privacy of her own home. She may then order them directly from the shop's computer, using her personal credit card. Far away a computer-controlled order-picker in a fully-automated warehouse may even load them on to a robot truck, programmed to find its way to her door.

But people will still want to buy things instantly and where they can try them on. There will be fewer actual goods in the store, and far more emphasis on display. There will be holograms of outdoor scenes on beaches and in gardens, and designers will use them to create new colour and furnishing schemes for the customer's kitchen or bathroom. Here, too, there will be no need for actual money. All purchases will be made with personal credit cards.

Shops will become places where people go to relax, to enjoy themselves and to see the latest gadgets and fashions. Occasionally, they will even buy something and carry it home in an old-fashioned shopping bag!

Will department stores look like this?

1. When she enters the store, the customer inserts her personal credit card in a computer terminal which checks her credit-worthiness. Security officers watch for any attempt at fraud.

2. On the right is an information display screen, showing the layout of the store.

3. Beyond this, a 3-D hologram display of an outdoor scene draws a crowd.

4. A more conventional display in the fashion area is surrounded by actual clothes – some articles must still be tried on!

5. On the first floor there is a first-aid point.

6. An escalator leads to the second floor.

7. Children can be left safely in the play area on this floor.

8. Video-telephones in soundproof booths are provided for the use of customers.

9. Moving display screens advertise special offers.

10. The restaurant and relaxation area has hardly changed!

11. A customer is using his personal credit card to buy a suitcase at a purchase point.

12. A moving pavement carries people around the edge of the first floor.

13. If the customer wishes to take her purchases with her, she has to insert her credit card again to receive them at the checkout point. From here, robot carts run to the car- and hoverjet-park attached to the store.

▲ This vast indoor shopping centre is built outside a city and is the size of a small town. It has its own enormous carpark and is easily reached from the nearby motorway.

Reference Section

General Information

If you are thinking of a career in a department store, you will find that most large stores offer thorough training programs. In fact, retail selling is one of the few areas left where a person can advance to an executive level regardless of educational background.

Although a college education is desirable for those interested in higher-level jobs, opportunities abound at all levels for those who have the proper talent and ambition. Retailing provides a wide range of jobs, and an individual can advance within one segment of a store's operation, or he or she can learn how to run an entire store.

What job areas are available? In merchandising there are sales workers, merchandise clericals, assistant buyers, buyers, and merchandise managers.

The promotional department has the responsibility of generating interest in the store's goods. Copywriters, commercial artists, layout artists, window trimmers, display specialists, and designers perform this task. As part of this overall promotional effort the public relations department serves as the store's link to the public. More and more, stores are reaching out to their surrounding communities to establish ties. The department's writers and speakers not only project a favorable image of the store, they also offer community assistance.

The operations department is in charge of security, maintenance, shipping and receiving, and inventory. There are engineers, guards, clerks, porters, repair workers, and even, at times, carpenters and plumbers.

Who does the hiring? The personnel department's role is to find competent people and place them in the right jobs. This division works closely with the store's other departments, especially with departmental managers.

Finding and training employees is only part of the job of this department. Executives in this area must also know how to deal with labor rela-tions problems and understand laws pertinent to hiring practices, wages, and working conditions. Not all people in this area are executives. Stenographers, secretaries, and assistants and specialists in related fields are part of this staff.

The finance, or control, section disburses money, whether it be for paying employees or for buying store goods and supplies. This section has bookkeepers, clerks, accountants, secretaries, credit interviewers, and finance executives.

Here, as in many departments, there is an increasing reliance on computers. There are numerous opportunities for the person who has the aptitude to program, process, or transfer data from electronic data processing machines.

The young person interested in a career in retailing should realize that any experience in any aspect of a department store's operation is extremely valuable. Many schools have chapters of the Distributive Education Clubs of America (DECA). These and similar organizations offer programs that combine business studies with work in a department store. Any direct work experience—be it part-time work during holidays or during summer vacation—is an important stepping-stone.

Students hoping to pursue a career in retail sales should be good in mathematics. Also, the ability to speak clearly and be at ease with people is a prime factor in considering employment with any department that deals directly with the public. But there are many behind-the-scenes jobs: in store operations there are many positions in specialized maintenance work and other manual labor.

Any training at a vocational school that concentrates on your area of interest is recommended. Moreover, many junior colleges offer courses in retailing. Such studies could serve as a foundation for a career, and they would give an individual time to investigate the varied opportunities that stores provide.

Training and Qualifications

The positions listed below are just some of the jobs offered in retailing, but they are especially reflective of the work done in department stores. Many jobs, such as those in personnel, control, and store operations, are similar to such jobs at any large company. Managerial positions exist in each of these areas.

Sales Workers

The federal Bureau of Labor Statistics notes that there are nearly 3 million sales workers employed in the United States. Most of these sales personnel work in department stores, where courteous and efficient service does much to satisfy customers and to build a store's reputation.

The sales worker should know his or her merchandise and be able to answer questions concerning it, put potential customers at ease, and create an interest in the product.

Retail sales workers make out sales or charge slips, receive cash, and give change and receipts. They also handle returns and exchanges of merchandise and keep their work areas neat. In smaller stores they help

order merchandise, stock shelves, mark price tags, take inventory, and prepare displays.

Entry and Salary Employers prefer to hire high school graduates. Any experience in a DECA program, or one similar to it, should prove helpful.

Persons interested in sales jobs should apply at the personnel offices, where they are likely to be interviewed and, sometimes, given an aptitude test. New workers often work in housewares, notions, or another department where the customer needs little assistance.

The starting pay is often the minimum wage, but employees can usually purchase store goods at sizable discounts. Since Saturday is a busy day in retailing, employees usually work that day and have a weekday off. It is frequently necessary to work extended hours, including evenings, during busy holiday periods. The key point to remember is that the sales worker is the store's direct link to the customer. The sales worker's job is a vital one, and the person who is successful in that role can readily advance.

Merchandise Clericals

This job is a good foundation for someone who hopes to become a buyer. The merchandise clerical keeps track of the flow of goods, making sure that his or her department has enough items in supply and that orders are being filled as specified and processed through shipping. Inventory information is often supplied by computer, so the ability to interpret such data is pertinent.

Entry and Salary The pay is often minimum wage or slightly higher, but the job affords a good chance for promotion.

Buyers/Merchandise Managers

Entry and Salary This job is usually attained after an apprenticeship as an assistant buyer. The apprentice watches, questions, and listens to the buyer as he or she purchases the goods sold in a particular field.

The buyer's job is often thought of as a glamorous, fast-paced life of style. Sometimes it is, but not every buyer deals in high fashion.

Buyers must keep informed of changes in products and have a keen sense of anticipation with regard to consumers' interests. Buyers attend trade shows, visit manufacturers' showrooms, and meet with manufacturers' representatives to place orders for merchandise.

Buyers should have a good sense of what items will sell, and how quickly, and at what profit. Although sales workers and assistant buyers can help buyers to "feel the public's pulse," buyers themselves often spend time on the sales floor to discover responses to products. Buyers must also study marketing reports and read trade journals to keep abreast of trends.

The merchandise manager does what the buyer does, but he or she does it for several departments. Someone with a demonstrated and continued success as a buyer is a prime candidate for merchandise manager. There is no guarantee that such a person will succeed, but a good buyer is a person whose risks have paid off. Such a person is willing to make bold, quick, and fruitful decisions, and that's the merchandise manager's ticket to success.

Computer technology plays a major role in this area, since many cash registers are connected to a computer, or point-of-sale terminal, which records up-to-the-minute inventory information.

DECA programs are very helpful as an introduction to buying. Many a good buyer began as a stock clerk or sales worker without any college

training. However, new buyers will find a college degree increasingly necessary, especially in marketing or purchasing. Many trade schools offer pertinent courses.

Although courses in merchandising or marketing may help in getting a first job, most employers are willing to train graduates from other fields. The training, which usually lasts several months, combines classroom work with short rotations to various jobs in the store. Training as an assistant buyer lasts for about a year. After several years as a successful buyer, a person can be promoted to merchandise manager, but all of these promotions are dependent on the person's growth and the company's needs.

Most buyers earn between $17,000 and $28,000 a year; merchandise managers earn considerably more. These figures depend on the product involved, the store's sales volume, and the length of time the worker has served. Buyers often receive bonuses for exceptional performances.

Merchandise managers and buyers often work more than 40 hours per week, the pace is hectic, and the pressure is intense. But the person eager to succeed in department store retailing can advance to a top managerial position via this difficult but rewarding route.

Copywriters/Artists

Copywriters in the advertising department write ads, and artists design and illustrate them. Many stores contract with advertising agencies to do this work, but the goal is the same: get people interested in buying the product.

The copywriter and artist, often under the pressure of a deadline, must consult with merchandise managers, buyers, production workers, and radio and television personnel.

risky work. But this position can be richly satisfying and a challenge to one's creativity.

Entry and Salary Many employers prefer to hire college graduates as copywriters; a degree in advertising, marketing, business, journalism, or liberal arts is sometimes required. But, as with other phases of the department store, work experience may be more important than educational background.

The artist, who creates the visual impact of the ad by selecting photographs, by drawing illustrations, and by selecting typefaces, may have studied in an art school, or, like the copywriter, he or she may have worked "up the ladder" by doing an assortment of jobs.

Nevertheless, imagination and creative talent are necessary in these jobs, and the copywriter and the artist must be able to quickly focus their talents on how best to attractively present the product. Lower-level jobs in advertising pay about $10,000, but higher-level positions can pay $35,000 or more. A combination of sharp talent, creativity, and diligence can give the person in advertising a profitable career.

Display Workers

Display workers develop exhibits that attract customers and encourage them to buy. Display workers should possess a keen imagination, a knowledge of color harmony, composition, and marketing techniques.

Using hammers, saws, spray guns, and other tools, display workers often build many of the props themselves.

In large stores that employ many display workers each person may specialize in a particular activity, such as carpentry, painting, sign-making, or setting up interior or window displays. If there is a display director, he or she coordinates the activities of all the display workers and confers with store managers, artists, and others.

Entry and Salary Most display workers start as window trimmers and learn their trade through informal on-the-job training. Gradually, they are given more tasks to perform, and if they have artistic talent, they begin to plan simple designs for displays.

When hiring inexperienced workers, employers look for high school graduates trained in art, woodworking, drawing, or merchandising. Many employers seek college graduates who have studied art, interior decorating, fashion design, or related subjects.

Freelance work is also a means to employment, but this is highly competitive, especially for beginners.

The starting pay for a display worker ranges from about $2.85 to $4.25 an hour. Experienced workers earn from $150 to $275 weekly, but display directors can earn $25,000 or more yearly.

Display workers often must work overtime; also, building and installing props can be very awkard and

Useful Words

Accessories Articles, such as scarves, belts, jewelry, and wallets, that accent or complete one's wardrobe.

Clearance A final sale that clears out remaining stock.

Fixtures Facilities used to display goods to be sold: shelves, counters, racks, bins, gondolas, etc.

Gondola A free-sanding display fixture that can be approached from all sides.

Hard goods For the most part, goods that are not worn: tools, television sets, appliances, etc.

Import An item that is not made in the United States.

Inventory The goods or merchandise on hand, or stock; also, to count the number of goods on hand.

Item One piece of merchandise.

Layaway A system whereby an item is reserved after a customer makes a small deposit. The customer picks up the item after completing payments over a specified time.

Markdown A lowering of the price of an item, or the amount of reduction from the original selling price.

Markup An increase in the selling price, or the amount added to the cost price.

POS terminal A point-of-sale terminal, or cash register, linked to a computer to record sales and inventory data.

Seconds Goods with minor defects or slight damage, or goods which are soiled. These items are in otherwise good condition. They are almost always sold at reduced prices; also called **imperfects.**

Shrinkage Unaccountable losses, due to theft or inventory errors.

Soft goods Merchandise that is worn.

Traffic The movement and flow of merchandise or customers.

Traffic item Merchandise that is in constant demand.

References

The following sources can be consulted for further information on jobs in department stores. Of course, the stores themselves are the best places to get in touch with.

National Retail Merchants Association, 100 W. 31st St., New York, NY 10001

American Advertising Federation, 1225 Connecticut Ave. N.W., Washington, DC 20036

United States Office of Education, Division of Vocational/Technical Education, Washington, DC 20202

National Association of Trade and Technical Schools, 2021 L St. N.W., Washington, DC 20036

Book List

Bodle, Yvonne G., and Joseph A. Corey. *Retail Selling,* 2nd ed. New York: McGraw-Hill, 1977.

Ferkauf, Eugene. *Going into Business: How to Do It by the Man Who Did It.* New York: Chelsea House, 1977.

Greeif, Edwin. *Store Talk.* Belmont, CA: Fearon-Pitman, 1979.

Mahoney, Tom and Leonard Sloane. *The Great Merchants,* new and enlarged edition. New York: Harper & Row, 1974.

Marcus, Stanley. *Minding the Store.* New York: New American Library, 1975.

Occupational Outlook Handbook. Washington: Bureau of Labor Statistics, U.S. Department of Labor, published every two years.

Wilinsky, Harriet. *Careers and Opportunities in Retailing.* New York: E.P. Dutton, 1970.

Acknowledgments

Key to the position of illustrations: (T) top; (C) centre; (B) bottom; and combinations, for example: (TR) top right; (CL) centre left.

Artists
Kate Charlesworth/Jenni Stone: 20, 33 (T), 35, 39
Bob Harvey/David Lewis Management: 14-15
Hayward Art Group; 4-5, 10, 13, 28, 31, 33 (B), 36, 37 (L)
Patrick O'Callaghan: 37 (R)
John Shackell: 10, 17, 25, 30, 40
Peter Watson: 42

Photographs
Aerofilms Limited: 43
Aktiebolaget Nordiska Kompagniet: 21 (B), 25 (R)
Antiference Limited: 27 (BR)
Associated News: 29
The Dutch Dairy Bureau: 22
Trevor Fry: 11 (T), 17
Trevor Fry/Macdonald: jacket (front), 2, 16 (TL), 18, 21 (TR), 26
Richard and Sally Greenhill: 16 (B)

Harvey Nichols: 21 (TL)
London Fire Brigade: 32 (B)
Magasin, Copenhagen: 8
John Lewis Partnership: 6 (t) and (B), 7 (BL), 9 (BR), 12 (L) and (R), 13 (B) and (T), 35 (BR), 37 (TL), 38 (T)
Fran Miller: 27 (BL)
Fran Miller/Macdonald: 7 (T) and (BR), 9 (TL), (TR) and (BL), 10, 11 (B), 23 (T) and (B), 24, 25 (L), 27 (TL) and (TR), 30, 31, 32 (T), 34, 35 (T) and (BL), 36, 37 (TR) and (C), 38 (B), 39 40, 41, 44, 45, 46, jacket (back)
Penguin Books Limited: 23 (CR)
John Sims: 28
Syndication International: 16-17
R. Twining and Co. Limited, Andover: 23 (CL)

The Author and Publishers would like to thank the following companies for their help and assistance in the preparation of this book: Bentalls Ltd, Bourne and Hollingsworth Ltd, Debenhams Ltd, Jaeger, Liberty and Company Ltd, Selfridges Ltd and The John Lewis Partnership.

Index

1 2 3 4 5 6 7 8 9 10—CAD—85 84 83 82 81 80